GEOGRAPHY MATTERS IN
ANCIENT GREECE

Melanie Waldron

heinemann
raintree

T0040569

© 2015 Heinemann Raintree
an imprint of Capstone Global Library, LLC
Chicago, Illinois

To contact Capstone Global Library, please call 800-747-4992, or visit our web site www.capstonepub.com

All rights reserved. No part of this publication may be reproduced or transmitted in any form or by any means, electronic or mechanical, including photocopying, recording, taping, or any information storage and retrieval system, without permission in writing from the publisher.

Edited by Helen Cox Cannons and Jennifer Besel
Designed by Philippa Jenkins
Original illustrations © Capstone Global Library Limited 2015
Illustrated by HL Studios, Witney, Oxon
Picture research by Jo Miller and Pam Mitsakos
Production by Helen McCreath
Originated by Capstone Global Library Ltd

Library of Congress Cataloging-in-Publication Data
Waldron, Melanie.

Geography matters in ancient Greece / Melanie Waldron.
    pages cm.—(Geography matters in ancient civilizations)
Includes bibliographical references and index.
ISBN 978-1-4846-0963-7 (hb)—ISBN 978-1-4846-0968-2 (pb)—ISBN 978-1-4846-0978-1 (ebook) 1. Greece—Historical geography—Juvenile literature. 2. Human geography—Greece—Juvenile literature. 3. Greece—Civilization—To 146 B.C.—Juvenile literature. I. Title.
  DF35.W35 2015
  938—dc23   2014013378

This book has been officially leveled by using the F&P Text Level Gradient™ Leveling System.

Acknowledgments
We would like to thank the following for permission to reproduce photographs: Alamy: © Nikos Pavlakis, 13; Corbis: © Ali Kabas, 22, NASA, 5, © National Geographic Society, 33, 35; Dreamstime: Ashwin Kharidehal Abhirama, 39, © Ivanbastien, 30, © Panagiotis Karapanagiotis, 17; Getty Images: De Agostini/DEA/G. DAGLI ORTI, 19, Hulton Archive/Print Collector, 11; iStockphoto: © kharps, 38, © sborisov, 4, © sneska, 36; Shutterstock: Alex Andrei, 10, AridOcean, relief map (throughout), Andrey Starostin, 16, cybervelvet, 20, Dimitrios, 32, Fedor Korolevskiy, 25, Free-lance, 28, Jerric Ramos, 27, Nadezhda1906, 41, Panos Karas, 7, 24, Vladimir Korostyshevskiy, cover, Tanjala Gica, 12; Superstock: IML, 9, Universal Images Group, 21. Design Elements: Nova Development Corporation, clip art (throughout).

We would like to thank Brian Williams for his invaluable help in the preparation of this book.

Every effort has been made to contact copyright holders of material reproduced in this book. Any omissions will be rectified in subsequent printings if notice is given to the publisher.

All the Internet addresses (URLs) given in this book were valid at the time of going to press. However, due to the dynamic nature of the Internet, some addresses may have changed, or sites may have changed or ceased to exist since publication. While the author and publisher regret any inconvenience this may cause readers, no responsibility for any such changes can be accepted by either the author or the publisher.

Contents

Some words are shown in bold, **like this**. You can find out what they mean by looking in the glossary.

Who Were the Ancient Greeks?

The ancient Greek **civilization** lasted from around 2000 BCE to 30 BCE. During this time, there were a few different groups that ruled. Each ruled over slightly different **territories**. The ancient Greeks were not ruled over by one leader, but they all shared a way of life, beliefs, and traditions.

The ancient Greek civilization had a large impact on how the modern world developed. Historians know a lot about it and are still learning more.

Historians have learned a lot about ancient Greek **culture** from some of the amazing stone buildings that they built, such as the Acropolis in Athens.

4

AEGEAN SEA

This **satellite** image shows the Aegean Sea and the land surrounding it. This is where the ancient Greek civilization was.

How was Greek civilization affected by geography?

The mainland of ancient Greece was hilly and mountainous. It had a long, rugged coastline. There were also over 1,400 islands in the Aegean Sea that were part of ancient Greece. The mountainous land with large amounts of coastline had a big effect on the way the Greeks lived. It affected where they could live, how they could travel, what they could farm, and their openness to attack. They had to make use of the natural **resources** that the land provided, they had to grow enough food to survive, and they had to find enough water to drink and water their crops.

DID YOU KNOW?

The Aegean Sea was at the center of ancient Greek civilization. It is about 380 miles (612 kilometers) long and 186 miles (299 kilometers) wide. Its deepest point is about 11,627 feet (3,544 meters). Its total area is about 83,000 square miles (215,000 square kilometers).

How do we know about ancient Greece?

The Greeks built temples, theaters, and sports arenas out of stone. Stone is durable. It does not rot like other building materials such as wood. Some stone buildings and the ruins of others are still standing today. We can study these buildings as well as **artifacts** that have been found in and around ancient Greek buildings and sites. These artifacts include vases, sculptures, and jewelry.

DID YOU KNOW?

One of the many inventions in ancient Greece that has lasted into modern life is the theater. Most cities in ancient Greece had a theater, where plays were shown. However, unlike today, only men and boys were allowed to be actors.

There are some ancient Greek shipwrecks in the Mediterranean Sea that also contain useful information about the Greeks. Some of the **cargo** has survived, sealed inside clay pots. Although very few pieces of writing have survived, the Romans made copies of ancient Greek writing that have lasted better. We can use all of these things to learn about and understand the Greek civilization.

How did ancient Greece help to shape the modern world?

The ancient Greek civilization influenced people across Europe, helping to shape western civilizations in areas such as art, science, **philosophy**, and government.

There were many educated Greeks whose studies became the start of modern thinking. Herodotus and Thucydides were two of the very first historians, interested in studying the past. Some Greek philosophers such as Socrates, Plato, and Aristotle created ideas about how the world worked. Greek artists had the idea of creating very realistic forms of art. Doctors such as Hippocrates started to look for scientific reasons for illness and disease.

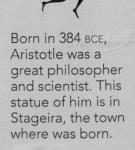

Born in 384 BCE, Aristotle was a great philosopher and scientist. This statue of him is in Stageira, the town where was born.

Where in the World Was Ancient Greece?

Ancient Greece was centered on the Aegean Sea, part of the Mediterranean Sea. It included the islands within the Aegean Sea and the lands around its edges. It also included the land where modern-day Greece is, and the land to the east, which is modern-day Turkey.

This large map shows the lands of ancient Greece, and the small map shows the location of modern-day Greece.

Illyria

Macedonia

Chalcidice

Mount Olympus

Epirus

Thessaly

ANCIENT GREECE

Thermopylae •

Aegean Sea

Thrace

Ionia

Corinth •
• Athens

• Mycenae   Attica

• Miletus

Naxos

• Sparta

Thera

Mediterranean Sea

N

0	50	100 Miles
0	50	100	150 Kilometers

CRETE

DID YOU KNOW?

The highest mountain in Greece is Mount Olympus, at 9,570 feet (2,917 meters) high. The ancient Greeks believed that Greek gods lived here, above the clouds. Zeus, the head of the gods, ruled over them.

Homer, a famous ancient Greek writer, wrote that the top of Mount Olympus had "pure upper air."

What is the physical geography of the area?

The mainland of ancient Greece was the large **peninsula** of land that runs from the southeastern corner of Europe down into the Mediterranean Sea. The sea surrounds this strip of land on three sides. The peninsula is connected at the north end to the rest of Europe. Lots of smaller peninsulas span out from the mainland peninsula, and there are many small **natural harbors** along the coast.

The mainland is mostly rugged, hilly, and mountainous. The mountains cover around 80 percent of the mainland area. Although they are not high, the mountains are steep and the slopes are covered with bare rock.

The islands in the Aegean Sea range in size. Some, such as Crete and Rhodes, are large and have many towns. Some are tiny **islets** that are too small to live on. Some of the islands are made up of mountains, **extinct** volcanoes, and rocky cliffs. Others have more gentle slopes that people can farm.

What was the climate like?

The climate of ancient Greece was very similar to today—hot, dry summers and cooler, wetter winters. The northern mountainous areas can be very cold, with freezing temperatures. The climate affected the crops that Greeks could grow as well as their housing and clothing.

Ancient Greeks had to find ways to farm and live in hot, dry weather and on steep, rocky slopes.

What natural hazards were there?

The area around the Aegean Sea has had many earthquakes throughout history. There have also been some volcanic eruptions. There was a huge volcanic eruption around 1500 BCE, when the volcano on the island of Thera (now known as Santorini) exploded. It blew away a large part of the island and covered the rest in ash.

Earthquakes happen when the large **tectonic plates** that make up Earth's outer layer slip against each other. There is a small plate called the Aegean Sea plate, which sits under most of the Aegean Sea and the southern part of Greece. When it slips against the larger plates that surround it, earthquakes can happen in the area. These earthquakes are usually quite small, but there have been far larger ones. In 464 BCE, a devastating earthquake destroyed the ancient Greek city of Sparta and 20,000 people were killed.

This is how an artist imagined what the island of Thera looked like after the huge volcanic eruption around 1500 BCE.

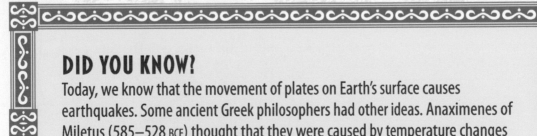

DID YOU KNOW?

Today, we know that the movement of plates on Earth's surface causes earthquakes. Some ancient Greek philosophers had other ideas. Anaximenes of Miletus (585–528 BCE) thought that they were caused by temperature changes inside Earth. Aristotle (384–322 BCE) thought that **air currents** on Earth's surface affected the inside of Earth, and so caused earthquakes.

How Did Ancient Greece Begin?

The first important European civilization was the Minoan civilization, which began around 3000 BCE. The Minoans lived on the Mediterranean island of Crete. They built much of their civilization on trade, and traded with people living on other islands close to Greece. They also traded with ancient Egyptians. They **exported** things like food, wood, and wine that they could produce on Crete. They **imported** things like gemstones and metals that they did not have.

The Minoans lived in settlements around large palaces on Crete. Each palace had its own king who ruled over the local area.

The volcanic eruption on the island of Thera was so powerful that it tore away much of the island and spread ash as far away as Egypt and Israel.

What happened to the Minoans?

Historians think that the volcanic eruption on Thera may have started the end of the Minoan civilization. Thera was only 62 miles (100 kilometers) from Crete, and the explosion would have created a huge **tsunami** (wave of water) around 39 feet (12 meters) high. This would have crashed onto the coast of Crete and destroyed many communities.

The eruption would also have thrown out so much gas and ash that it would have affected the climate for many years. This is because the gas and ash in the sky blocked some of the heat and light from the sun. This small change in temperature over many years caused poor harvests. When the Minoans came under attack from the Mycenaeans, from Greece, they were too weak to fight back.

Who ruled after the Minoans?

The Mycenaeans started living on the southern mainland part of Greece from about 1600 BCE. They lived in small, separate city kingdoms that spoke the same language and shared the same culture. The cities were built on high ground, and their palaces and forts had high stone walls. By using the natural features of the landscape and their natural resources of stone, they were able to protect themselves from attackers.

This map shows the location of the Mycenaean lands. They took over Crete, which was previously ruled by the Minoans.

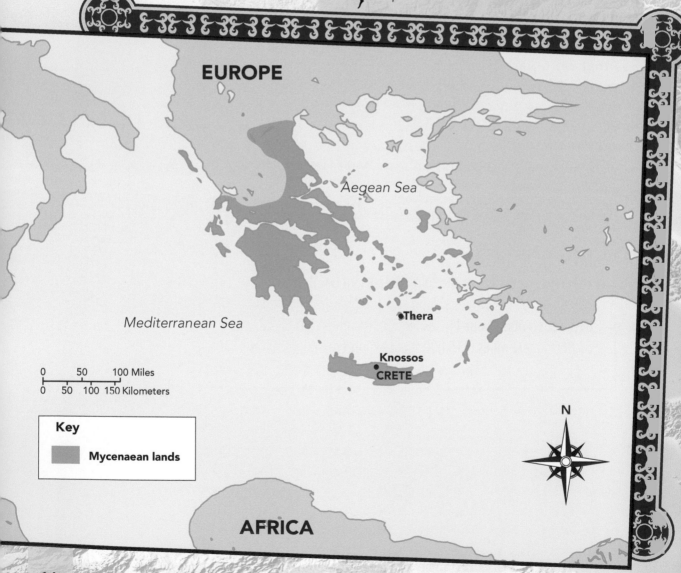

EUROPE

Aegean Sea

Mediterranean Sea

•Thera

Knossos
•
CRETE

0   50   100 Miles
0 50 100 150 Kilometers

N

Key

Mycenaean lands

AFRICA

The Mycenaeans were warriors and sailors who traded around the Aegean Sea and beyond. After they defeated the Minoans, they took control of the Minoan trade routes. The Mycenaeans imported gold, ivory, amber, timber, and metals such as copper and tin. They exported oil, wine, cloth, weapons, and vases.

What happened to the Mycenaeans?

From around 1250–1200 BCE, the Mycenaean civilization became weakened. This may have been because of some years of poor harvests. There would have been little food to go around, and many people would have been affected by **famine**. Around this time, many cities began building stronger defenses. Historians think this was because groups of Mycenaeans began attacking each other to steal food.

Some Mycenaean people started moving out of their kingdoms to other areas, traveling overland and on large ships. Many Mycenaean cities were abandoned. Some were then destroyed by earthquakes. Much of the Mycenaean culture was lost.

DID YOU KNOW?

The period in ancient Greece from around 1100 to 800 BCE is called the Dark Ages. There were no powerful rulers in this period, the population declined, and most people lived simple lives farming the land. There are no written records from this time, and not much is known about it.

How Did Ancient Greece Change After the Dark Ages?

The civilization of ancient Greece started to grow in strength again around 800 BCE. The population grew larger at this time. As the population grew, villages and towns became bigger.

Corinth was a powerful city-state. These are the remains of the Temple of Apollo in Corinth.

What were city-states?

Groups of villages that were near each other in the mountainous areas formed strong trading links. They began to merge together as they grew bigger. Eventually, these settlements became **city-states**. They were separated from other city-states by the difficult mountainous **terrain**. This terrain made it hard to travel and communicate. The geography of the area kept the city-states apart.

Hundreds of different city-states formed, some more powerful than others. Each had its own government and **capital city**. The capital city was usually on the highest ground in the area. Although they were independent from each other, the city-states shared the same language, culture, and religion. This gave them a common identity and created strong links between them.

Which city-states were the strongest?

Corinth was a powerful city-state, located near many trade routes in the Mediterranean. From around 550 BCE, Athens became more powerful and wealthy. It was in the region of Attica, which was rich with **minerals** like silver and marble. Athens grew wealthy through trade, the population increased, and it became the largest city-state. At the same time, Sparta grew in strength. It was ruled by warriors, and every man had to be a soldier.

This is a Greek statue of a Spartan soldier. Spartan soldiers were feared across the Greek **empire**.

17

How did ancient Greece's influence spread?

The Greeks started to influence areas around the Mediterranean Sea from around 740 BCE. Greeks had already been moving to these areas during the Dark Ages. They were escaping famine and, when the population began to grow again, overcrowding. When the city-states started forming, they were sometimes at war with each other. Some Greeks traveled by sea to other areas, such as the south coast of France and the east coast of Spain, to escape this. The areas where these people settled became known as Greek **colonies**, where the people lived as they had done in Greece. Soon they became independent states, just like the city-states on the mainland.

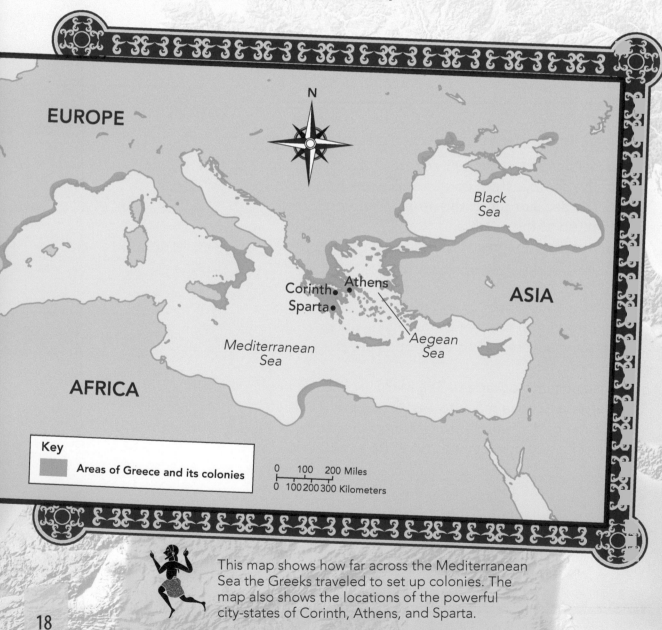

This map shows how far across the Mediterranean Sea the Greeks traveled to set up colonies. The map also shows the locations of the powerful city-states of Corinth, Athens, and Sparta.

DID YOU KNOW?

The Greeks built many temples in Syracuse, on the island of Sicily. Unlike other Greek temples made from marble, these temples were made of limestone and **terracotta**. This is because there is very little marble to be found on Sicily.

Beautiful vases, similar to this one, were exported from the Greek mainland. They were often filled with olive oil, and they were traded across the colonies in exchange for grain.

Were the colonies important for trade?

The colonies became important coastal **trading posts** where goods could travel in and out of the areas farther inland. One of the most important goods traded in these colonies was grain. Many of Greece's city-states had grown so big that they could not grow enough grain to feed everyone. Athens, for example, had to import around two-thirds of its grain.

What Natural Resources Did Ancient Greece Have?

There was not much flat and **fertile** land to farm in Greece. However, the Greeks did manage to farm some of the land.

Olive trees grew well on the steep, stony slopes.

DID YOU KNOW?

Many people worked on the land, and even the smallest farms would have a slave to do the hard work, such as digging the soil, planting and harvesting crops, and tending to the animals. Slaves were often children who had been abandoned by their parents. Slaves could be bought and sold.

This Greek vase shows people picking olives. They packed the olives into nets and crushed them between stones to extract the valuable oil.

What crops did ancient Greeks grow?

Greek farmers could grow crops on the areas of flatter land around the coast and in valleys between mountains. They even used some of the steep, stony slopes for growing olive trees or for grazing sheep and goats.

On the flatter land, barley and wheat were important crops, used to make bread and porridge. The seeds were sown in October and harvested in April or May. Other crops were beans, lentils, onions, leeks, and garlic.

Which crops were especially valuable?

Olives and grapes were also important crops. Olive oil was used for cooking, making medicines, and as fuel for lamps. Grapes were crushed to make wine. The Greeks placed a high value on olive oil and wine, as did other groups of people around the Mediterranean. They exchanged other goods for olive oil and wine.

What did the sea provide?

Most Greeks ate some kind of fish and seafood every day. Tuna, mackerel, squid, and octopus were very common. Around the coasts, fishing was a big industry. Fishermen used small wooden boats and caught their catch with nets and spears. This was hard and tiring work. However, it was not too dangerous because the Mediterranean Sea is usually calm, especially around the coasts.

This statue shows Poseidon, god of the sea and brother to Zeus. Many fishermen worshipped Poseidon.

What minerals were mined in ancient Greece?

The land of ancient Greece contained different types of minerals. The Greeks used minerals to make everyday items and special treasures. They used clay to make pottery and also to make some medicines. Artists used colored minerals, such as red hematite, to make **pigments**. The Greeks used emery, a hard stone found on the island of Naxos, for filing and shaping other stones. Sharp blades and ornaments were made from obsidian, a glass-like stone, and buildings were made from limestone and marble.

This map shows some of the natural resources that the ancient Greeks were able to use.

Aegean Sea

N

Key

G	Gold
S	Silver
I	Iron
C	Copper
L	Lead
M	Marble

0	50	100 Miles
0	50	100	150 Kilometers

Greeks mined metals such as gold and silver in the mountains of northern Greece. Silver was also mined in Laurium, near Athens. Iron and copper were used for making tools.

DID YOU KNOW?

Deep shafts were dug around 262 feet (80 meters) into the ground to reach the precious silver at Laurium. Slaves—adults and children—were sent down these shafts. Conditions were terrible, and many slaves died doing this work.

Ancient Greek society really started to flourish around 500 BCE. For many years before this, Greece had been under attack from Persian people from western Asia.

How was ancient Greece ruled?

The city-states had their own governments, and they ruled in different ways. In 508 BCE, Athens started a new system of rule. It was called a **democracy**, which means rule of the people.

All the people of Athens belonged to one of 10 different tribes. Each tribe chose 50 **citizens** to join the Council, which consisted of 500 people altogether. The Council suggested new laws, which were then discussed by the Assembly.

The Assembly was a gathering where every citizen of Athens was allowed to speak and vote. The Assembly met once every 10 days.

The Assembly in Athens met here, on Pnyx Hill. There had to be 600 citizens present before a meeting could begin.

DID THE ANCIENT GREEKS USE MONEY?

At first, people in ancient Greece did not use money. Instead, they **bartered** for goods, exchanging one thing for another. Historians think that coins were invented in the city-state of Lydia, on the eastern side of the Aegean Sea, in the 7th century BCE. The idea of coins then spread to the rest of ancient Greece.

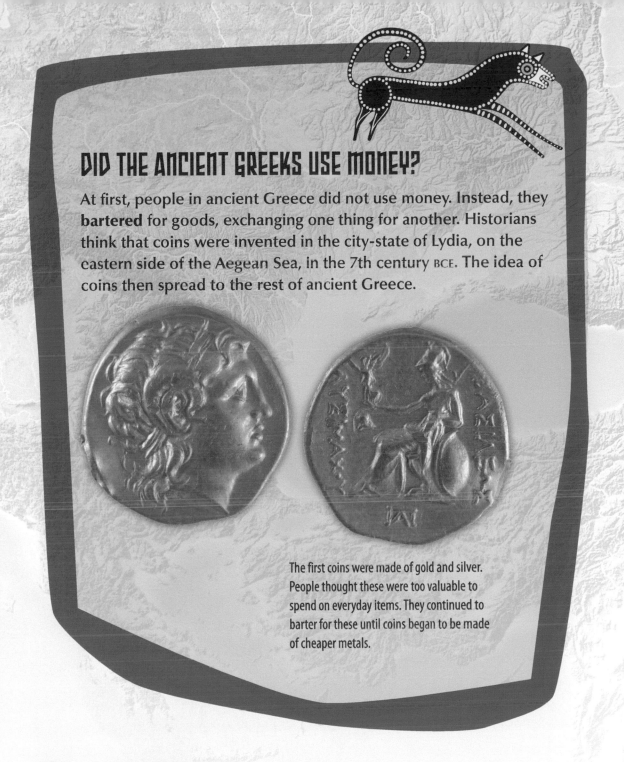

The first coins were made of gold and silver. People thought these were too valuable to spend on everyday items. They continued to barter for these until coins began to be made of cheaper metals.

Who was a citizen?

A citizen in a city-state did not just mean a person living there. Only men born in a city-state could be citizens. Women, slaves, and men born outside the city-state could not be citizens.

What were ancient Greek towns and cities like?

Most towns and cities had an acropolis in the center. This was an area of high ground where there was a temple for the god of that town or city. Greeks thought that some natural features had special religious meanings. Many caves, **springs**, and hilltops were chosen as sites to build temples and **shrines**. In these places, people left gifts for gods and nature spirits or asked for their help.

Many towns and cities were protected by stone walls, with gates across the roads leading in and out. The main road in usually led straight to the *agora*—a large, open space in the center where people gathered for markets, meetings, games, and socializing.

What were ancient Greek buildings like?

Houses and other ordinary buildings were made from mud bricks, with stone bases and clay tiles on the roofs. There were wooden shutters on windows to keep out the hot sun. Most houses were arranged around the sides of a courtyard.

TOWN PLANNING

Many older towns and cities grew in a haphazard way around the central acropolis, agora, and council buildings. But some newer towns were planned more carefully, with streets following a grid pattern. An **architect** named Hippodamus of Miletus designed the new harbor town of Piraeus. This was an important town because it was the closest **port** to Athens, and many goods came in and out of this port.

Greeks built important buildings, such as theaters and temples, out of stone. The Greeks liked simple, elegant designs. Many buildings had a row of columns at the front that supported a horizontal beam across the top. Often there was a triangular section on top of this beam. The stone was beautifully decorated and carved. This classical Greek design of building was copied by the Romans and can be seen in many places around the world today.

The U.S. Capitol Building, where the U.S. Congress meets in Washington, D.C., is based on a classical Greek design. It was built in the early 1800s.

How Did the Ancient Greeks Travel?

Traveling overland in Greece was difficult because of the steep and rocky mountains. Carts could not travel on the narrow mountain paths. Everything had to travel on the backs of donkeys or mules. Most people had to travel on foot, since only wealthy people could afford horses to ride.

Coastal roads

Where the land was flatter around coastal areas, it was possible to build some roads. Here, horses could pull chariots, and donkeys, mules, and oxen could pull farm carts. Because Greeks had wheeled transportation in these areas, it was easier for army equipment, food, and goods to be moved around. It was also a lot easier for people to travel farther.

Donkeys, with their small, hard hooves, were ideal for carrying goods along the steep, rocky mountain paths.

Some roads had grooves cut into them for the wheels of chariots and carts to run along. This made for a smoother and faster ride. Only the grooves had to be tended to and repaired, rather than the entire width of the road. However, it also meant that chariots and carts had to be built to the same width so that their wheels would fit into the grooves.

This diagram shows the grooves that the Greeks used. The wheel grooves were cut into the durable strips of stone laid into the road surface.

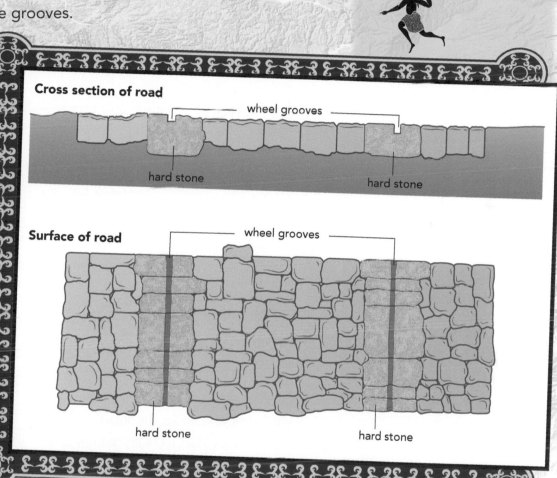

Cross section of road

wheel grooves

hard stone   hard stone

Surface of road

wheel grooves

hard stone   hard stone

How did the poor roads affect the city-states?

Roads were poor, with deep potholes and trenches. In the countryside, travelers were often attacked by bandits. Since traveling overland was difficult and dangerous, travel by sea was the best option for moving people and goods around Greece. This meant that the city-states that became the biggest, wealthiest, and most important—including Athens, Corinth, Syracuse (Sicily), and Miletus—were the ones that had seaports.

Why did the ancient Greeks travel by sea?

Sea travel was so common because it was quicker than traveling overland and because it made trading easier. The mainland was a long peninsula with the sea on three sides. There were city-states in and around the Aegean Sea. The rest of the states were reached by sailing over the Mediterranean Sea. Many towns and cities were located along the coastal edges of the land, and there were lots of natural inlets and harbors where ships could dock to load and unload their goods.

As is true today, many ancient Greek settlements were on the flatter land along the coast, and sea travel was very important.

DID YOU KNOW?

There was a very narrow strip of land joining the southern part of mainland Greece to the rest of the mainland. A leader of Corinth in the 6th century BCE named Periander thought of an ingenious way to make money from this. His slaves built a stone track across the narrow strip of land, and he charged money for ship-owners to have their boats dragged across the track, saving them a long sea journey. Today, there is a canal that boats can use.

Why was sea travel dangerous?

People often paid merchant ships to carry them as passengers along with the goods the ship was carrying. However, these ships' sailors often robbed their passengers. Also, ships could be attacked by pirates or crash onto rocks.

How did ancient Greeks navigate the seas?

Most sailors preferred to sail close to the land. They didn't have compasses and had to rely on their knowledge of the coast, the sun, and the stars to guide them. Some sailors were skilled at making maps. Some even learned to navigate their way around the islands in the Aegean Sea by looking at how the clouds usually formed in the area. Others got to know the different smells that drifted from each island!

What Was Ancient Greek Culture Like?

The quality of life for people in ancient Greece very much depended on their status, and if they were a man or a woman. For rich men, for example, there was much to enjoy about life—through education, arts, and sports. The one aspect of life that was equal for everyone was religion.

There were many different Greek gods and goddesses. The 12 most important of these were thought to live on Mount Olympus. Greeks built temples in their honor, and different towns and cities had temples for different gods and goddesses. People offered prayers and gifts and asked for help.

This is a statue of the goddess Athena. Athens is named after her.

LIFE FOR ANCIENT GREEK WOMEN

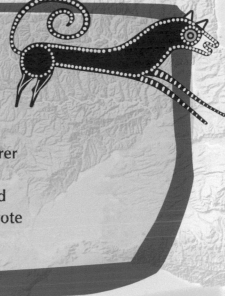

Women in Greece led different lives from citizens and other men. They were usually married by the age of 15. Then, they mostly stayed at home and ran the household. Poorer women got out a little more, but only to collect food and water. Very few women had paid jobs, and no women were allowed to vote or take part in politics.

Did children go to school?

Boys from wealthy families went to school. They learned to read and write, and to do math using an **abacus**. Some boys went on to study more and became philosophers, scientists, historians, and inventors. Girls had to stay at home. If their mothers could read, some lucky girls were taught this skill by them.

This painting shows women spinning wool and weaving cloth, jobs that were mostly done by women.

What items of art could ancient Greeks enjoy?

There were skilled sculptors in Greece who crafted amazing sculptures and patterns out of stone and marble. Greece had lots of high-quality marble, and much of it came from quarries on the islands of Paros and Naxos. Clay was another material that artists used, found all over Greece. It was used to make vases, plates, and cups. The metals that were mined were used to make statues, ornaments, and jewelry.

Why did ancient Greeks hold sports festivals?

The Greeks held sports festivals to honor their gods and goddesses. These festivals included events such as running, wrestling, and discus throwing. The Olympic Games were in Olympia, to honor Zeus. The Panathenaic Games were held in Athens, to honor Athena. These two festivals were the most famous games and were held every four years.

This is one of two ancient Greek bronze statues, called the Riace Warriors, that were found on the seabed near southern Italy in 1972. They had lain there for 2,500 years, protected by the soft sands of the seabed in that area.

Although traveling was difficult in Greece, many people came to these games. Some people traveled from as far away as Spain and Egypt to attend. The leaders of any warring city-states would call a **truce** while the games were happening.

These Greek athletes are competing in a race. Their prize would be fame and a crown made of olive branches.

DID YOU KNOW?

The ancient Olympic Games were a large spectacle. In addition to the athletes and the spectators, there were lots of traders and people providing services. The area had very little fresh water, and many people and donkeys were kept busy carrying pots of water to the site.

What Ended the Ancient Greek Way of Life?

The powerful city of Athens went to war with the strong city-state of Sparta in 431 BCE. This war lasted until 404 BCE, when Athens finally surrendered. By this time, around one-third of the population of Athens had been killed by a **plague**. Historians think that this disease was carried into the city by rats that had come from ships docking at the port of Piraeus. The fall of Athens was the start of the decline of ancient Greece.

Where was the power held after Athens?

Sparta took control after Athens fell, but it was not able to hold onto it. In 371 BCE, the city-state of Thebes took control of Greece. Meanwhile, the kingdom of Macedonia to the north of Greece was growing in strength. In 359 BCE, Philip II became king of Macedonia. He started invading land to the east and south, and in 338 BCE, he took control of all of Greece. The independent rule of the city-states came to an end.

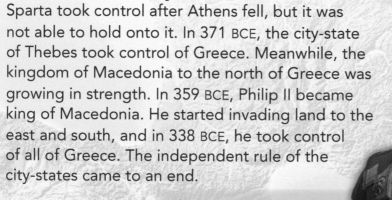

This is a statue of Philip II. Some historians think he was killed by one of his wives, Olympias.

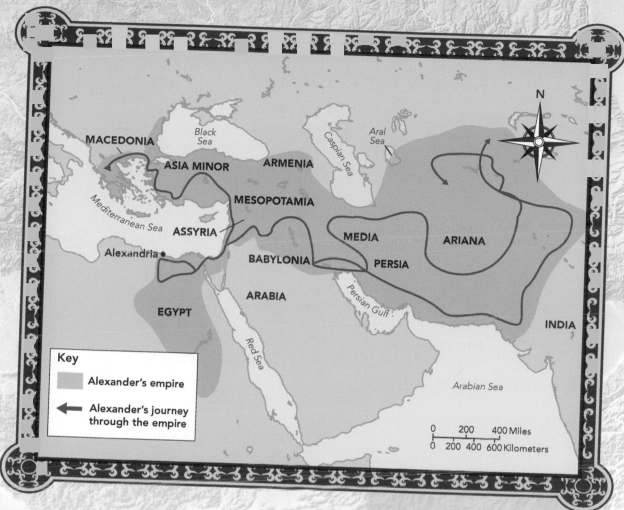

The map includes the following labels:

MACEDONIA
Black Sea
Aral Sea
ASIA MINOR
ARMENIA
Caspian Sea
N
Mediterranean Sea
MESOPOTAMIA
ASSYRIA
MEDIA
ARIANA
Alexandria
BABYLONIA
PERSIA
Persian Gulf
ARABIA
Red Sea
EGYPT
INDIA
Arabian Sea

Key
Alexander's empire
Alexander's journey through the empire

0   200   400 Miles
0   200 400 600 Kilometers

Who was Alexander the Great?

Alexander the Great was Philip's son, and he became king in 336 BCE, after Philip died. He created a huge empire to the east, as far as India. He was crowned King of Egypt and Great King of Persia.

This map shows the empire created by Alexander the Great before he died in 323 BCE.

DID YOU KNOW?

With the spread of Alexander's empire, the influence of ancient Greece spread, too. Greek became the language that traders used. Greek art, architecture, and town planning became common in these lands.

What happened after Alexander the Great died?

Control of the huge empire passed to Alexander's two sons. A group of generals ruled for them, as they were too young, but the generals fought each other for power. This left the empire in ruins, and most of Alexander's family was killed, including his sons. By 281 BCE, the empire had split into three parts, ruled by three generals:

- Antigonus ruled most of Greece and Macedonia.
- Seleucus ruled a huge empire from the east side of the Aegean Sea to India.
- Ptolemy ruled Egypt and the coastal areas of the eastern Mediterranean.

DID YOU KNOW?

Ptolemy II built a huge library in Alexandria that contained writings from Greece, Egypt, and elsewhere. It became a great place of learning. The library preserved a lot of knowledge and understanding of Greek culture for many centuries.

This is the Bibliotheca Alexandrina, built near the site of Ptolemy's library in Alexandria. It was completed in 2001 and was inspired by the original library.

Cleopatra was the last queen of Egypt before the Romans took control. She was also the last Greek ruler of the area that had been taken over by Ptolemy.

When did the Romans take over ancient Greece?

Arguments and wars in the three Greek-ruled empires made them weak. At the same time, the Romans were becoming stronger. After 200 BCE, they began conquering more and more lands. They defeated the leaders in Greece in 168 BCE. The final part of land that had once been under Greek control to fall was Egypt, which came under Roman control in 30 BCE.

Was Geography Important in Ancient Greece?

The shape of the land in ancient Greece had a huge effect on the way the civilization developed. City-states were independent from each other because of the mountainous terrain of the mainland. Although they were united by language and culture, they were often at war with each other and ruled in different ways.

The long length of seacoast and the many islands of Greece meant that sea travel and trade were very important. Many cities were close to the sea, and leaders built huge fleets of military ships called triremes. These defended the Greek coastline and attacked other coastlines. The Greek colonies around the Mediterranean Sea allowed Greek ideas to spread.

Across the land, the climate varied. It could be cold and snowy in the northern mountains in winter, but very hot and dry in the summer. This affected what Greeks could farm in different areas. The Greeks grew many high-value crops such as olives and wine. These could be traded for everyday goods like grain.

DID YOU KNOW?

Ancient Greeks realized that building houses to face south was an excellent way to provide heat in the colder months. In the city of Olynthus in northern Greece, every house faced south in order to catch as much sunlight as possible. Solar heating is yet another legacy of ancient Greece!

Many people today visit places in Greece where ancient Greek buildings still stand.

The ancient Greek world was shaped by its landscape and climate, which influenced its civilization. Through trade and conquest, this was then spread to other cultures, far away from Greece itself.

Toward the end of the civilization, the huge size of the empire meant that Greek culture spread over a wide area. Much of it has been preserved for us to study and enjoy.

Quiz

1

How many islands are there in the Aegean Sea?

a) Over 700

b) Over 1,400

c) Over 2,100

2

How would the Greek mainland best be described?

a) Hilly and mountainous with lots of coast

b) Flat and vast with lots of coast

c) Hilly and mountainous, in the middle of a continent

3

What is the deepest point of the Aegean Sea?

a) Around 1,161 feet (354 meters)

b) Around 11,627 feet (3,544 meters)

c) Around 116,273 feet (35,440 meters)

4

How much of the Greek mainland is mountainous?

a) Around 20%

b) Around 50%

c) Around 80%

5

What is a peninsula?

a) A group of islands near each other

b) A piece of land surrounded on nearly all sides by water

c) A long, thin line of mountains

6

Where did Greeks believe their gods lived?

a) Mount Olympus

b) Mount Everest

c) The Valley of the Kings

7

Which island was blasted by a huge volcanic eruption in about 1500 BCE?

a) Crete

b) Naxos

c) Thera

8

Where were the Greek colonies?

a) In the deserts of North Africa

b) Around the coast of the Mediterranean Sea

c) Around the coast of the Red Sea

9

Which trees grew well on the steep, stony slopes of Greece?

a) Olive trees

b) Palm trees

c) Oak trees

10

How many citizens had to be present before an Assembly meeting could begin?

a) 6

b) 60

c) 600

11

Why did the Greeks hold sports festivals?

a) To raise money for the city-states

b) To honor their gods and goddesses

c) To make sure people stayed fit and healthy

12

Which civilization eventually took control of Greek areas?

a) The Egyptians

b) The Incas

c) The Romans

Glossary

abacus instrument with beads or other counters that slide along rods or in grooves, used for counting or calculating

air current large volume of air moving in one direction

architect person who designs buildings

artifact object made by a human

barter trade or exchange things without using money

BCE short for "Before the Common Era," relating to dates before the birth of Jesus Christ

capital city where a country or area is ruled from

cargo goods carried by a ship

citizen person who is a member of a country or city-state because of being born there or being accepted as a member by law

city-state self-ruling state made up of a city and its surrounding territory

civilization society that has reached a high level of organization and culture

colony place that is under the control of a distant country

culture language, ideas, inventions, traditions, and art of a group of people

democracy government in which the people have power, either in a direct way or through chosen representatives

empire group of countries or people ruled over by a powerful leader or government

export take to another country, usually to be sold

extinct no longer existing or active; an extinct volcano will not erupt again

famine time when there is not enough food to feed all the people living in an area

fertile able to produce and support plants such as farm crops

import bring in from another country, usually to be sold

islet tiny island

mineral substance in Earth that does not come from an animal or a plant

natural harbor section of coastline shaped in such a way that it provides a safe area of water where people can leave boats and ships

peninsula piece of land surrounded on nearly all sides by water and connected to a larger area of land by a usually narrow strip of land

philosophy study of the nature of life, truth, knowledge, and other important human ideas

pigment substance that is used to provide color

plague disease that spreads quickly and kills many people

port place where ships load or unload goods

resource something of value to humans

satellite spacecraft that orbits around Earth and gathers or sends back information

shrine sacred place that is devoted to a holy person or god

spring place where water emerges out of the ground

tectonic plate section of Earth's crust that can move against another section and cause earthquakes and volcanic eruptions

terracotta hard, brownish-red clay used to make sculptures, pottery, and ornaments

terrain natural shape and characteristics of the land

territory area of land marked by certain natural features or claimed by a group of people

trading post place where local products can be traded for goods brought from distant places

truce end of a war that is agreed upon by all groups that are fighting

tsunami very large, often destructive sea wave that can be caused by an earthquake or a volcanic explosion

Find Out More

Books

Chisholm, Jane, Lisa Miles, and Struan Reid. *The Usbourne Encyclopedia of Ancient Greece*. Tulsa, Okla.: EDC, 2007.

MacDonald, Fiona. *Ancient Greece* (100 Facts). New York City: Sandy Creek, 2013.

Pearson, Anne. *Ancient Greece* (Eyewitness). New York City: Dorling Kindersley, 2007.

Spilsbury, Richard. *Discover Greece* (Discover Countries). New York City: PowerKids, 2012.

Web Sites

FactHound offers a safe, fun way to find Internet sites related to this book. All of the sites on FactHound have been researched by our staff.

Here's all you do:

Visit www.facthound.com

Type in this code: 9781484609637

Places to Visit

The Metropolitan Museum of Art, New York
www.metmuseum.org
There are lots of different objects from ancient Greece in this museum's collection.

National Hellenic Museum, Chicago, Illinois
www.nationalhellenicmuseum.org
This museum explores the history and culture of Greece.

Tips For Further Research

Thera eruption
The island of Santorini today is very different from the island (then called Thera) that existed before the huge volcanic eruption in around 1500 BCE. See if you can find out about the eruption. How big was it? How did it change the shape of the island? Is there anything left of the volcano today?

Greek rivers
River travel was not a main form of transportation in ancient Greece. Do some research to find out why. Was it because of the weather, or because of the landscape, or a combination of both? Or was it because of something else?

Index